THE HONEY BEE PORTRAIT

By Nancy Ann Bowe

ENTER

Protect The Honey Bees

Healthy Pollinators...
Healthy Planet!

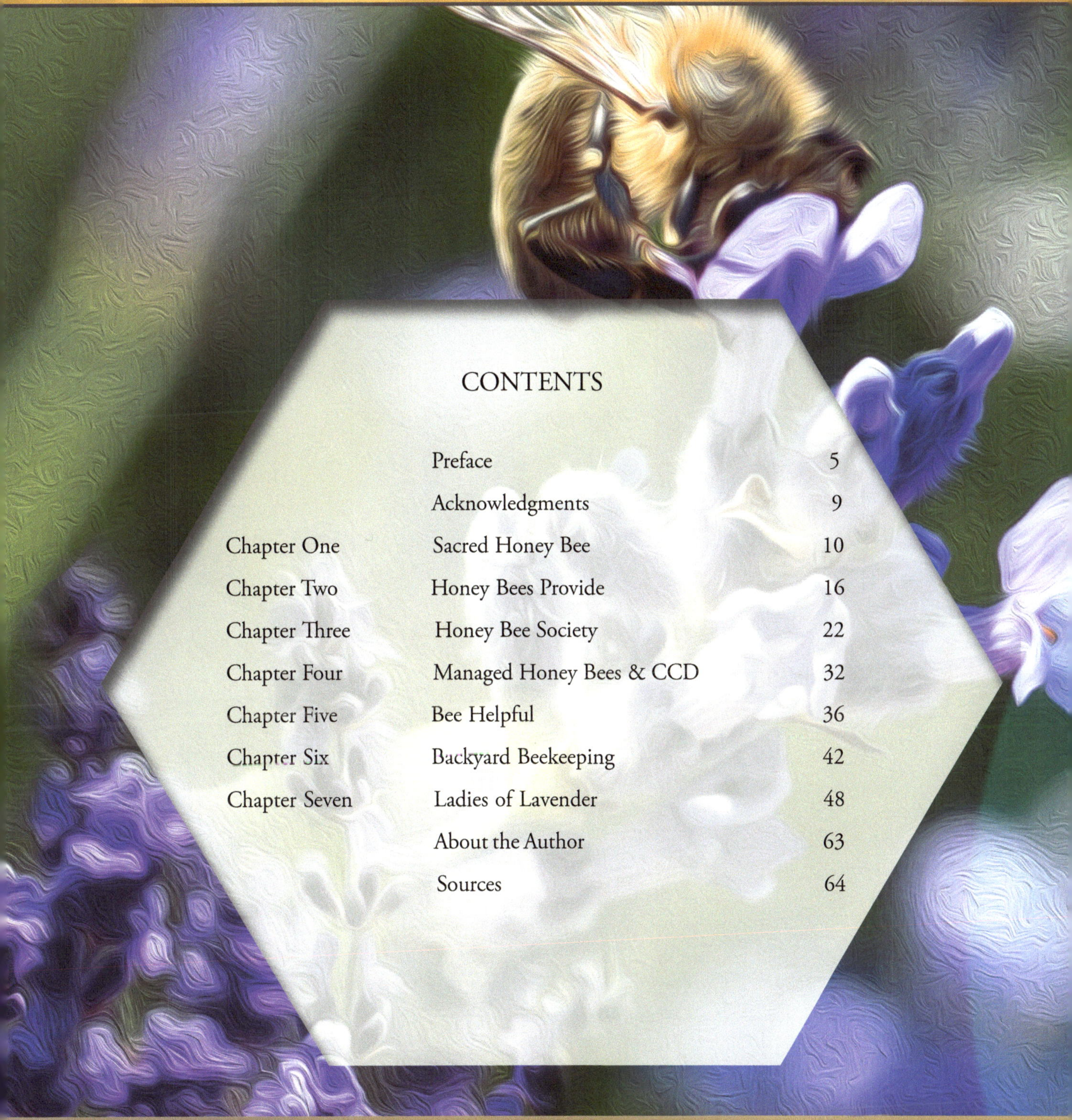

CONTENTS

	Preface	5
	Acknowledgments	9
Chapter One	Sacred Honey Bee	10
Chapter Two	Honey Bees Provide	16
Chapter Three	Honey Bee Society	22
Chapter Four	Managed Honey Bees & CCD	32
Chapter Five	Bee Helpful	36
Chapter Six	Backyard Beekeeping	42
Chapter Seven	Ladies of Lavender	48
	About the Author	63
	Sources	64

*"The bee is more honored than other animals, not
because she labors, but because she labors for others"*

- Saint John Chrysostom - (arch bishop of Constantinople, 347-407)

It's all about love, honor, and respect!

Preface

The object of this book is to share my love and respect of nature's most essential insect to the entire planet and all who inhabit it. That would be the honey bee. I am a graphic designer and photographer. I do not claim to be a specialist on the topic. However, I have always been fascinated by them, and I guess you could say obsessed!

After raising three sons, I enrolled in college to obtain my degree in Graphic Design. My obsession of photographing pollinators led me to want to learn more and more about them. This book was a part of my senior project/thesis for my Bachelor of Fine Arts Degree. More importantly, it is my way of helping these bees, who have been in decline over the last several years worldwide. By creating this book of my photography and graphics, I hope to help bring public awareness to the significance of the honey bees to humanity.

In the pages that follow, you can join me with what I have learned on my honey bee adventure. Take a closer look at the fascinating insects that for millions of years have worked hard in the background, almost unnoticed. They provide the world with some of the magnificent things life has to offer. Honey bees provide us with precious honey, they beautify our world by pollinating flowers, and more importantly, they pollinate one-third of our food supply! Let's all "bee friendly." It will make for a better world!

"If you want to gather honey, don't kick over the beehive."

- Abraham Lincoln

"*Bees do have a smell, you know, and if they don't they should, for their feet are dusted with spices from a million flowers.*"

– Ray Bradbury, Dandelion Wine

Acknowledge the ones you love!

Acknowledgments

First and foremost, I would like to thank my family for their love and support especially my sons, Robert, David, and Matthew for encouraging me to return to college to obtain my Bachelor of Fine Arts Degree in Graphic Design. Not to mention that I am not sure I could have survived college math without Matthew's patient tutoring!

Special thanks also go to my former professor Harold Naideau for mentoring me through my senior project/thesis by offering me his unlimited support and guidance but most of all for believing in me, keeping me on task, and for reminding me to wear protective gear while shooting bees!

I am grateful for my friend and cousin Kathy Vlacci, for going as far as holding lavender still in the wind for me to get the shot! Some of the shots were on a sweltering summer day, and tropical breezes were making the bees sway with the lavender plants. What you can't see is Kathy painstakingly holding the flowers steady. Thanks, Honey!

I would like to thank Serge and Susan Rozenbaum, owners of Lavender by The Bay in East Marion, New York, and Toni Bakker, a local beekeeper in East Moriches, New York for generously allowing me to pester their bees with my camera and for sharing their knowledge with me. Without their generous offers to help there would be no beautiful portraits of the precious subject.

Sincere thanks go to Ted and Jill Brandt for introducing me to Toni Bakker. She is a fantastic woman and backyard beekeeper that inspires me to one day keep my very own bees!

Last but not least, thank you, the reader, for taking the time to view my work and see the world of the honey bees as I saw it through my camera lens on my honey bee adventure!

Nancy Ann

Bees have evolved for over 100 million years. A fossil of a honey bee found in Southeast Asia remained preserved in honey. Honey has been held sacred since ancient times, due to the fact it resembled amber, and the bee has been used as a symbol of worship as far back as prehistoric times.

For example, discovered in the "Cave of the Spider" in Spain, is an old Mesolithic rock painting on the cave walls dating back to about 15,000 years ago. It depicts a person extracting honey from a beehive alongside a cliff.

Cave paintings are not the only evidence of bee and honey worship in prehistoric times. Also found was Aboriginal carvings of men carrying bags of honey located inside eucalyptus tree barks. Evidence also shows that beekeeping was a practice in Egypt as far back as 3000 BC or earlier.

Nowadays, it appears as though much of the respect and adoration for the sacred honey bee has gotten lost in modern times.

We live in a world of convenience where we can just walk into a supermarket and easily find shelves stocked with various types of honey and goods that the honey bees make possible. Maybe it is time to not take them for granted and show them the honor and respect that they deserve.

For fascinating information in regards to the ancient history of bees, check out "Beedazzled" articles written by author Andrew Gough at http://andrewgough.co.uk/articles_bee1/. The honey bee, according to Andrew, "is the real lost tradition and the forgotten goddess of the ancients."

Illustration by nancyongphotos.com ©2014

For so work the honey-bees, creatures that by a rule in nature teach the act of order to a peopled kingdom.

– William Shakespeare

This little honey bee is taking a well needed break before heading back out of the hive. They use the sun as their compass and can fly approximately two miles to forage for water, nectar and pollen.

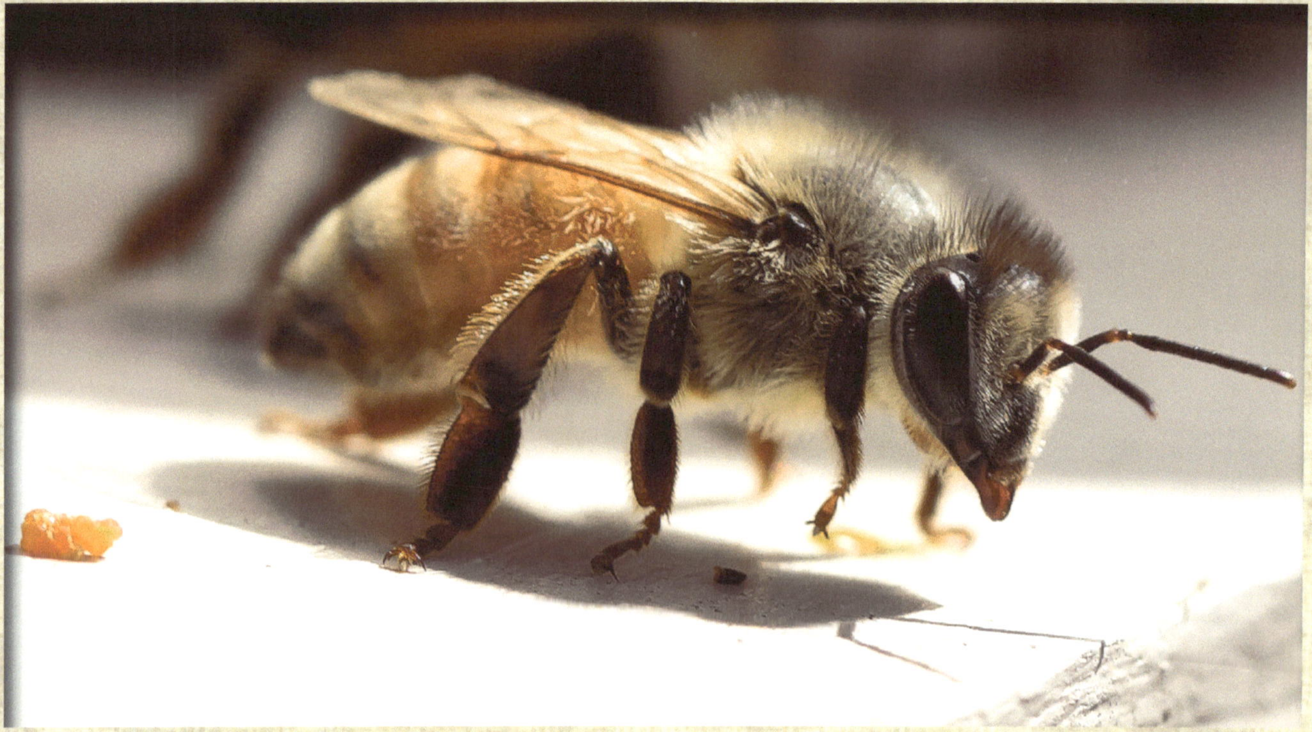

Honey bees hatch out of the honeycomb by chewing off the wax cap to join the colony and begin working. As soon as the newly hatched bee emerges, worker bees will come in and clean and prepare it for the queen to lay another egg. The queen requires a cell to be utterly immaculate before depositing an egg in it. If it does not meet her expectations, she will seek another cell.

Honey bee hatching out of the honeycomb cell. Development time for worker bees is approximately 21 days from egg to adult.

"Collaboration is the essence of life. The wind, bees and flowers work together, to spread the pollen."

– Amit Ray, Mindfulness Living in the Moment - Living in the Breath

Chapter Two

Honey Bees Provide

For centuries, honey has been referred to as

"the nectar of the Gods."

Honey bees are vital pollinators of crops as well as personal gardens, wildlife habitats, and orchards. According to the United States Department of Agriculture, approximately one-third of all of the foods consumed are pollinated by insects. Out of this one-third, honey bees are responsible for the pollination of around 80 percent of the crops.

Some of the crops honey bees pollinate are alfalfa, almonds, apples, apricots, avocados, blackberries, blueberries, cherries, cranberries, melons, grapes, grapefruit, nectarines, peaches, pears, persimmons, plums, pumpkins, raspberries, squash, strawberries, sunflowers, watermelons, and much more.

Honey bees also provide the human diet with nutritious, and medicinal honey. It is rich in vitamins, minerals, and is an antioxidant. Humanity has used honey for thousands of years for health and to provide the body with energy.

Other products that honey bees produce are bee pollen, propolis (bee glue), and royal jelly. Many products and supplements exist using these ingredients.

honey

"The sweetest honey
Is loathsome in his own deliciousness
And in the taste confounds the appetite."

– William Shakespeare (1564-1616) 'Romeo and Juliet'

> *"Tart words make no friends; a spoonful or honey will catch more flies than a gallon of vinegar."*
>
> – Benjamin Franklin

Making Honey

Worker bees that spend the day foraging come back to the hive and regurgitate nectar they gathered in their stomachs from the flowers into the mouths of the hive bees. Next, the hive bees regurgitate the nectar into a hive cell after they ingest it and break down the sugars.

To evaporate water from the processed regurgitated nectar, they fan it with their wings to thicken the liquid into honey. After the fanning process, they cap off the top of the cell with beeswax to seal it in for future use.

The busy bee has no time for sorrow.

- William Blake

Honey Bees Provide

Some of the foods that require bee pollination:

Adzuki Beans	Cauliflower	Green Beans	Persimmons
Alfalfa	Celery	Green Peppers	Plums
Allspice	Cherries	Guava	Pomegranate
Apples	Chestnut	Hazelnut	Prickly Pear
Apricots	Chili Peppers	Kidney Beans	Quince
Avocados	Clover	Kiwi Fruit	Rapeseed
Beets	Cocoa	Lemons	Raspberries
Bell Peppers	Coconut	Lima Beans	Red Peppers
Black & Red Currants	Coffee	Limes	Rose Hips
Blackberries	Congo Beans	Loquat	Safflower
Black Eyed Peas	Coriander	Lychee	Sesame
Bok Choy	Cotton	Macadamia Nuts	Star Apples
Boysenberries	Cranberries	Mango	Star Fruit
Brazil Nuts	Custard Apples	Mustard Seed	Strawberries
Broccoli	Cucumber	Nectarines	Sunflower Oil
Brussels Sprouts	Durian	Okra	Sword Beans
Buckwheat	Eggplant	Onions	Tamarind
Cabbage	Elderberries	Orchid Plants	Tangelos
Cactus	Fennel	Palm Oil	Tangerines
Cantaloupe	Figs	Papaya	Tomatoes
Caraway	Flax	Passion Fruit	Turnips
Cashews	Goa Beans	Peaches	Vanilla
Carrots	Tomatoes	Pears	

Chapter Three

Honey Bee Society

Honey bees live their lives in a very organized society with specific roles within the colony throughout their life. The various duties are foragers, guards of the hive, housekeepers, attendants, builders, health care attendants, cleanup crew, undertakers, and such.

Within the colony, there are three types of bees. First and foremost, there is only one queen per colony in the hive. The queen is the only female bee that has ovaries that fully develope. She lives the longest ranging from 3-5 years. She mates with several drones (male bees) only once and mating results in a lifetime of fertility. Per day, she lays up to 2000 eggs. When the eggs become fertilized, they turn into female worker bees. Left unfertilized, male drone bees will be born.

If a queen becomes ill or passes away, the colony will feed a selected larva royal jelly to produce a new queen. This royal jelly is only given to perspective queens and is high in vitamin B. It is made by a combination of honey, nectar, and pollen digested, and secretions from a nursing bee's gland located in their head.

Worker bees are unable to reproduce and are all female. During the winter they can live up to 4-9 month. However, they work so hard that the length of their life reduces to only six weeks. A hive can have anywhere from 60,000 to 80,000 bees during the summer season and most of which are the worker bees. During the winter months, this number can be diminished down to 30,000 or 20,000.

Last but not least, there is the male bee called the drone. The drone's principal duty is to mate in the air with a virgin queen from another hive. Unfortunately for him, he has a "barbed sex organ" that falls off resulting in his death after mating. They are small in number in the hives during the summer (approx. 300-3000), and they are kicked out of the hive in the fall so as not to take up unnecessary space in the winter. Also, drones do not sting due to the fact they do not have a barbed stinger.

HONEY BEE LIFE CYCLE

❶ EGG

Queen lays egg
in wax cell
Hatching = 3 days

❹ ADULT

21 Days
Total
Adult bee
leaves
cell

❸ PUPA

13 days

❷ LARVA

Feeding = 5 days

Honey bees build six-sided hexagonal cells made of wax to store honey, pollen, and larvae.

Honey Bee Queen

Royal Jelly

By feeding a virgin bee a protein secretion that worker bees have in glands in their head, a queen is born. As an adult bee, the worker bees continuously provide royal jelly to the queen. This particular diet makes her the only female bee that can reproduce. The other bees follow and protect her.

Honey Bee Queen

- ❦ There is only one queen per colony.

- ❦ The queen is the center of the world of the hive. She births all of the other bees in the colony.

- ❦ As ruler of the hive, she needs to mate. She takes flight to mate with ten to fifteen drones.

- ❦ Her only job is to mate and lay eggs. She lays around 2000 eggs per day. All of her other needs are taken care of by the workers.

- ❦ The queen has a unique pheromone. When it diminishes, the workers prepare another queen to take over.

- ❦ If the hive becomes too crowded, the queen will leave taking about 1/2 of the colony with her. This activity is known as swarming.

THE HONEY BEE PORTRAIT

"In the garden, birds sing, bees hum and the flowers and butterflies bewitch me. Every bug and beetle, petal and leaf grants peace to me in the present moment. As I tread upon emerald blades that gently sway below crystal skies, the garden unveils to me the philosophy of life."

– Amelia Dashwood

Worker Honey Bees

🐝 All worker bees are female and make up most of the colony's population.

🐝 Some are foragers (field bees) collecting pollen and nectar while others tend to the hive house bees.

🐝 Worker bees have barbed stingers and will only use them when they feel threatened. Once they use their stinger, they lose their life.

🐝 House bee duties include guarding, housekeeping, feeding, building honeycomb, organizing, making honey, tending to the queen and so much more.

🐝 The worker bees feed larvae royal jelly to produce a queen.

"Bees... by virtue of a certain geometrical forethought, knew that the hexagon is greater than the square and the triangle and will hold more honey for the same expenditure of material."

– Pappus, Greek Mathematical Works, Volume II: Aristarchus to Pappus

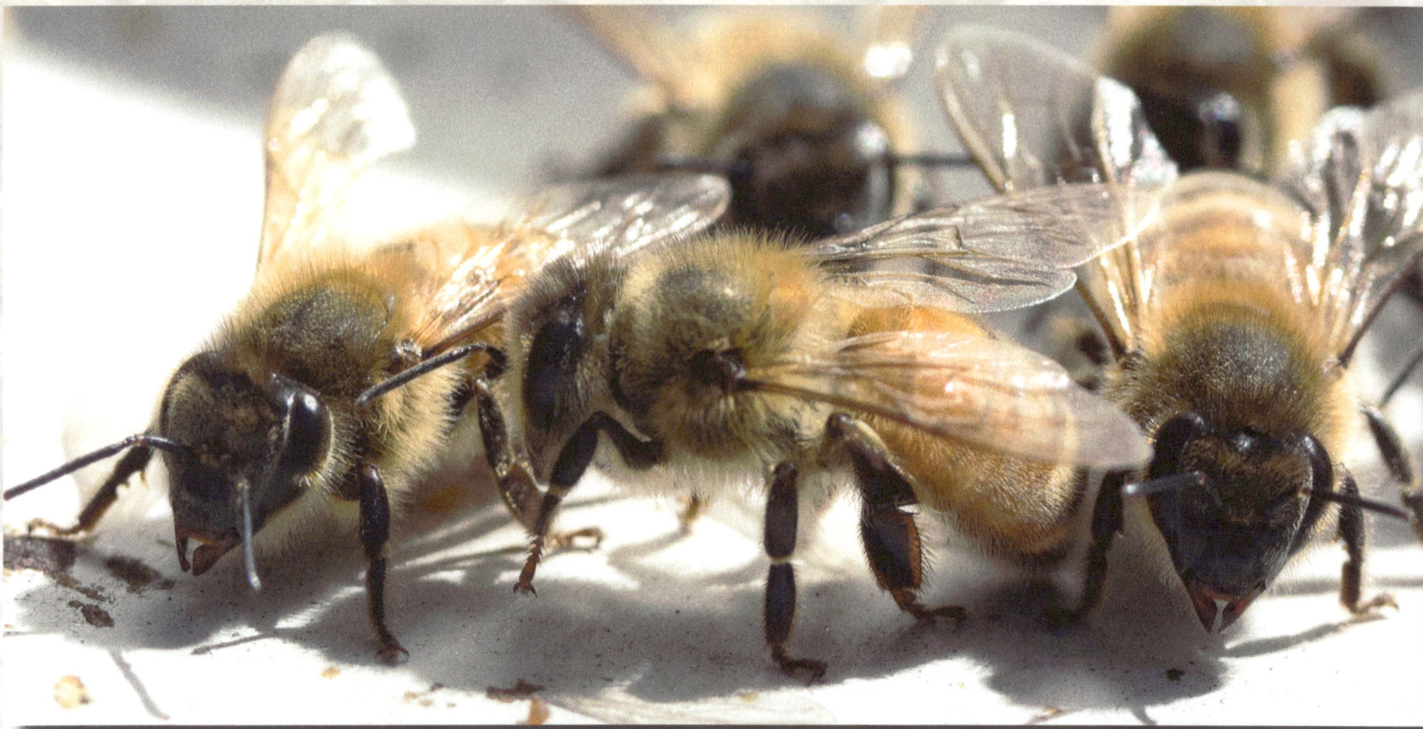

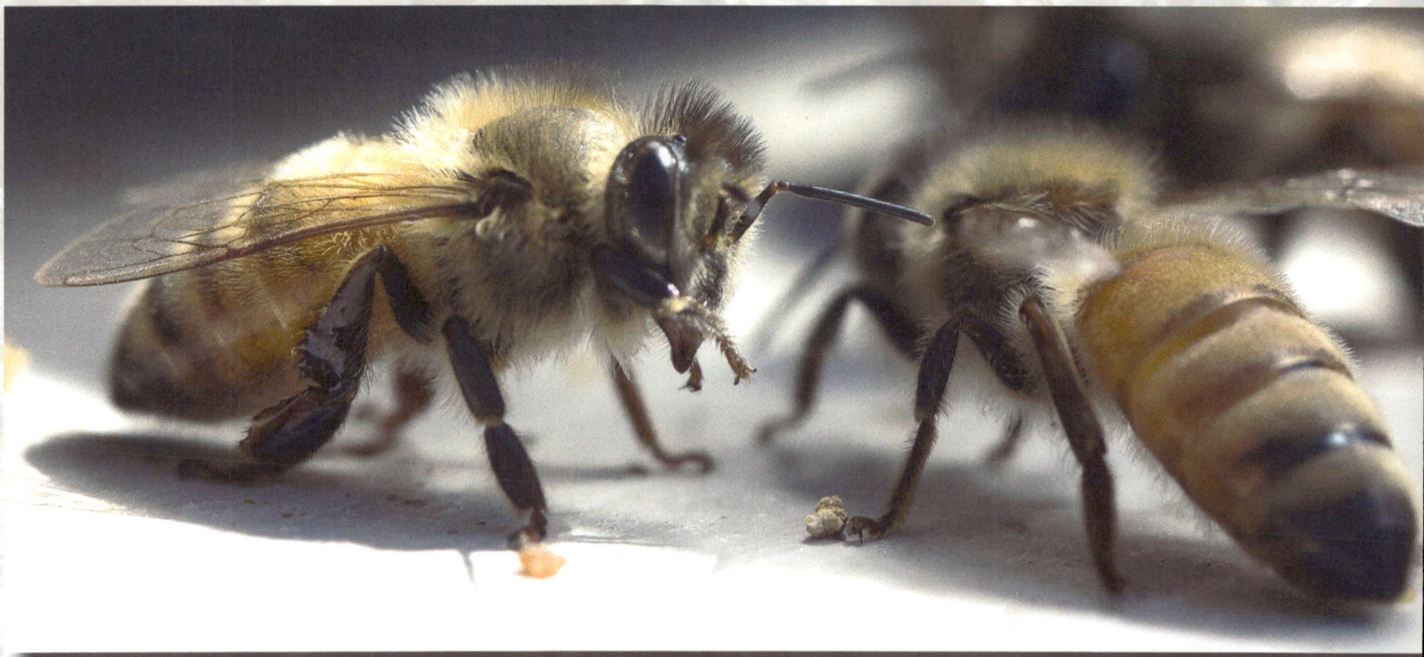

Honey Bee Drone

- ❧ Drones are male honey bees.

- ❧ They are not equipped with a stinger and make up a small part of the colony's population.

- ❧ Their life expectancy is about 90 days.

- ❧ Their only function is to mate outside the colony. Drones die right after mating with a queen in mid-air flight.

- ❧ Their eyes are twice the size of the queen and the worker's eyes.

- ❧ Drones are the product of an unfertilized egg. The worker bees feed and care for them.

- ❧ When cold weather sets in, the workers force the drones out of the hive to conserve their food supply.

Generally speaking, honey bees are not very aggressive while out foraging for nectar and pollen but they will sting to protect the hive or if they feel threatened.

Bee venom has been known to possess anti-inflammatory properties and used for pain therapy. Known as "Bee Sting Therapy," it has been practiced since ancient times. It is thought to boost the immune system, relieves pain and inflammation, and improves circulation. Unfortunately, some people can have a severe allergic reaction to bee venom so every precaution should be taken to protect themselves from being stung.

Many people around the world practice Apitherapy. Apitherapy is the use of all products produced by honey bees such as venom, honey, pollen, royal jelly, propolis, and beeswax for healing and well being.

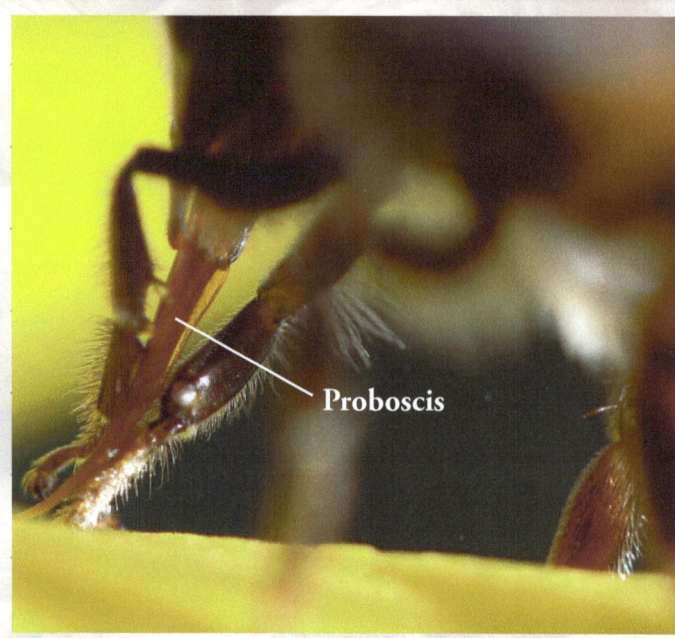

Proboscis

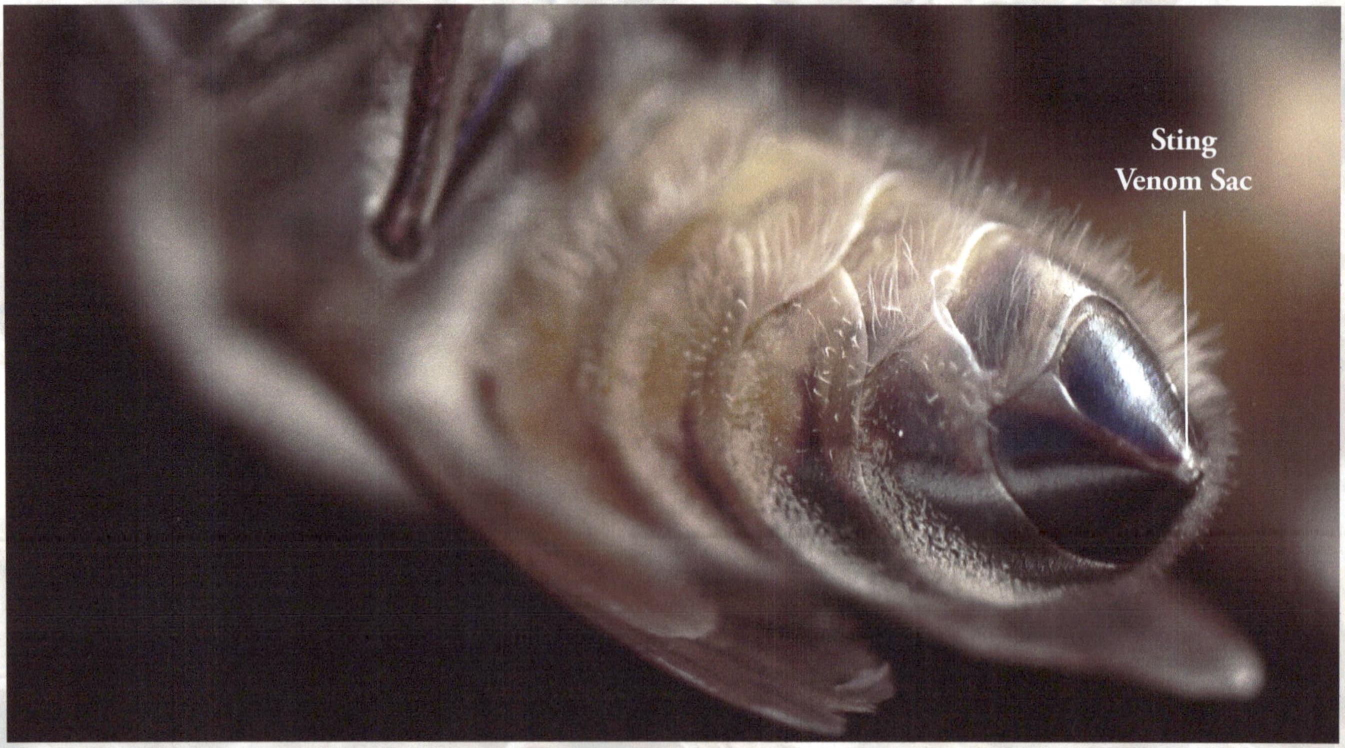

Sting
Venom Sac

Honey Bee Anatomy

Antenna

Ocelli

Thorax

Wings - 2 sets

Honey Stomach

Compound Eye

Mandibles

Proboscis

Abdomen

Stinger

Legs - six

Pollin basket

Honey bees chew with jaws known as mandibles. The proboscis is a tongue that is like a straw. They use it for sucking liquids, tasting, cleaning themselves, the hive, and the queen.

Chapter Four

Managed Honey Bees

Out of all of the approximately 20,000 species of bees, the honey bees are the most manageable in commercial agriculture to pollinate the crops. However, since 2006, commercial beekeepers have been reporting that their colonies have been mysteriously disappearing which caused their colonies to collapse. This phenomenon is known as "Colony Collapse Disorder (CCD)."

Colony Collapse Disorder was brought to public attention in the fall of 2006 by a beekeeper, David Hackenberg. He was a former president of the American Beekeeping Federation. In a letter to growers, Hackenberg reported a new disease he had never seen before that was afflicting his hives. His bees had utterly left and never returned to the colony. They were deserting the queen, young workers, larvae, and pupae. At that time, he lost over 2,000 of his 2,950 hives to the collapse disorder. He began hearing similar stories from other beekeepers.

Puzzled by the cause, and upset over the loss, he took some of his collapsed hives to Penn State to the team that later became known as the "CCD Working Group." Dennis van Engelsdorp, a state apiarist, and his colleagues at Penn State undertook the case studies of the mysterious colony collapse disorder.

Beekeepers across the country, and around the world, began to report mysterious bee "die-offs." Something strange was happening to their hives. One moment the honey bees seemed perfectly healthy, and within a few days, the colonies would collapse.

What sets CCD apart from past destroyers of colonies, is the absence of the dead bees; the abandoned brood and honey; the anxious behavior in the bees before vanishing, and the lack of predators moving into the empty hives. Ordinarily, predators such as other bees, wax moths, and hive beetles, would immediately go into the hive and steal the honey. It is as though insects sense that there is something wrong.

Maladies affecting commercial beekeeping have plagued the industry for many years. In fact, when the "Varroa" mite entered the United States in 1987, from the Far East, it wiped out millions of honey bee colonies. It was a devastating blow to professional beekeepers, putting a quarter of beekeepers across the country out of business. Varroa mites (and tracheal mites introduced in 1984) are still a problem in the industry today, and many beekeepers use pesticides to keep it under control. The parasite mites weaken the bee's immune system, causing diseases, and destroying colonies.

Continued on Page 34

Ways You Can Help

- PLANT A BEE FRIENDLY GARDEN

- SHOP AT LOCAL ORGANIC FARM STANDS

- SIGN A PETITION TO BAN THE USE OF NEONICITONOIDS

- LET DANDELIONS AND CLOVERS GROW IN YOUR YARD

- STOP USING COMMERCIAL PESTICIDES, HERBICIDES AND FERTILIZERS

- DONATE TO RESEARCH

- HOLD A FUNDRAISER

- BECOME A BACKYARD BEEKEEPER

Scientists have discovered cases where honey bees have died from mite infections, pesticides in the past. However, what has been extremely disturbing about the CCD dilemma is the fact that the bees are deserting the hives. It is instinct for the honey bee workers to provide for their colony and return. Finding the exact cause that would interfere with natural instinct has puzzled beekeepers, the government and research scientists for years.

Agriculture is a booming industry of growing crops in mass production to fill the needs of the consumers. Many beekeepers move their bees across the country by trucks from farm to farm, wherever needed. Many theorize that the constant movement of the bees causes them severe stress, which could weaken their immune system. Aforementioned could lead them to become susceptible to viruses. Unfortunately, that still does not explain the bizarre symptoms of CCD. Also, there were other speculated causes circulating over the last few years.

Some were questioning the rise in cell phone use, and others were blaming Earth's magnetic field movement, but no studies were conclusive.

Over the years, many beekeepers have been "pointing their fingers" at chemicals used by crop growers. The popular insecticides farmers use on crops pollinated by bees, such as fruits and vegetables, are neonicotinoids. In fact, France banned the use of these chemicals after they experienced a bee "die-off." French and Italian scientists did research and reported that "sub-lethal" amounts bees pick up in the fields could cause disorientation. These chemicals are still widely used in the United States.

Extensive research continues to try and pinpoint the exact cause of CCD, and the situation is being closely monitored to ensure that the cause and necessary treatments can be determined.

Colony Collapse Disorder

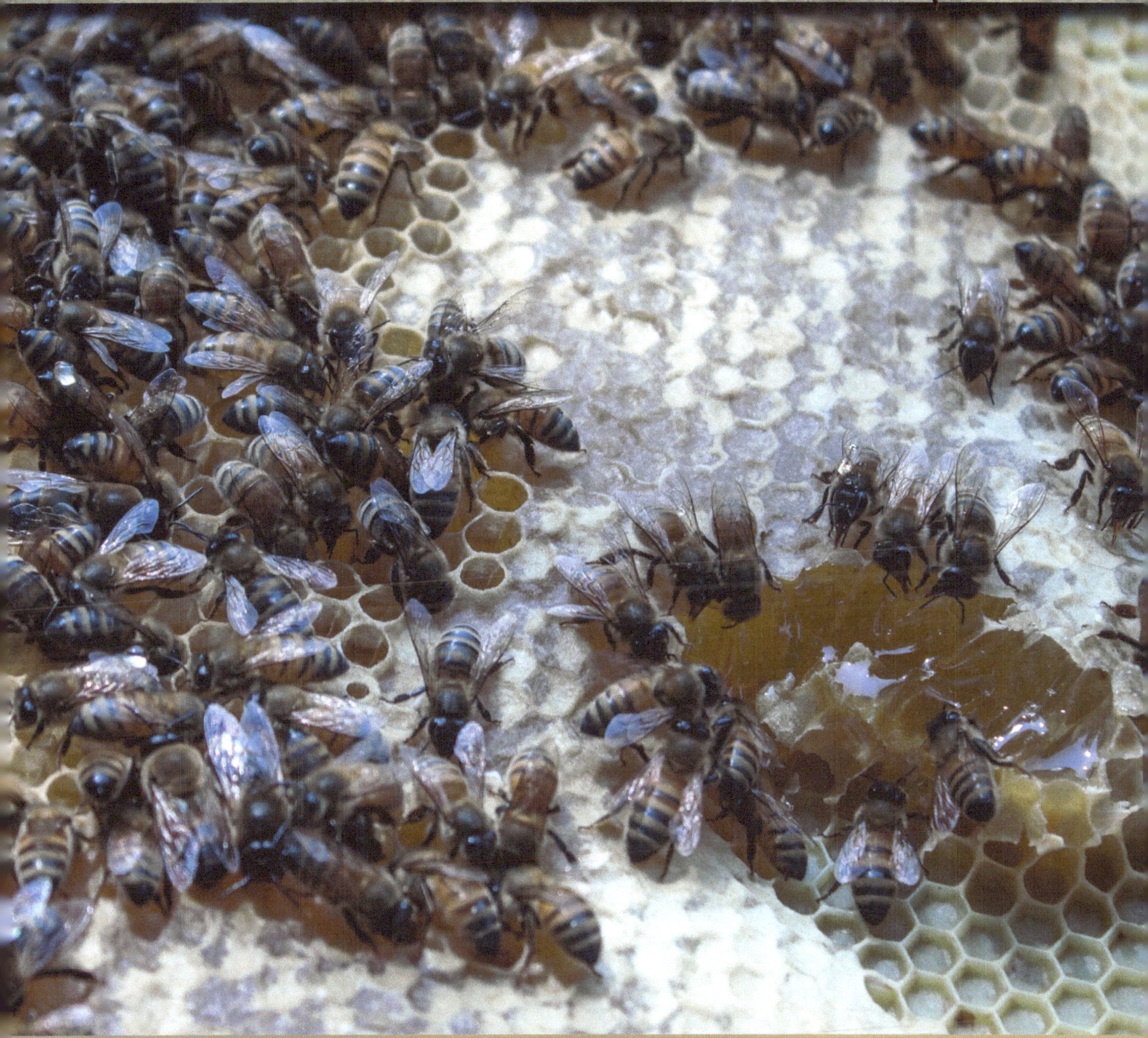

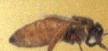

Chapter Five

Bee Helpful

One way in which we can all help the honey bees, as well as other pollinators, is to avoid using harsh chemicals on our lawns such as herbicides, commercial pesticides, and fertilizers. Honeybees love dandelions and clovers. Also, plant nectar-producing and native plants in your yard and create a bee friendly garden. One of the problems that native honey bees are facing today is that most people want well-groomed lawns, thus taking away a natural environment for the bees to thrive. Your local nursery can give you advice on which plants will do well in your area. It is also a good idea to plan out your garden so that different plants flower at various times to ensure that your little friends will have plenty to feast on all throughout the season.

Take part in educating the public on the value and importance of protecting the honey bees. Get involved in a fundraising event where the proceeds can go to a "save the honey bees" foundation. That would be a great way to get your community together to educate children and adults on the importance of pollination and to respect the honey bees, as well as all pollinators, and teach them about the critical role they play in the entire ecosystem.

Donate to a honey bee research foundation. You can research organizations on the web and find the one that you feel is best to receive a donation. For example, the largest and "most comprehensive state-supported apiculture facility in North America"

honey bee research facility is the Harry H. Laidlaw Jr. Honey Bee Research Facility at UC Davis. In fact, Haagen-Dazs donated $100.000.00 to UC Davis in 2008 and also started their own "save the honey bee" website. Also, Penn State's College of Agricultural Sciences is a leader in holistic pollinator health.

Shop at your local organic farmer's markets when the season allows. Fresh, locally-grown fruits and vegetables are safer, much healthier, and even taste better. While you are there, be sure to stock up on some local organic honey fresh from the honey bees! It is great to keep on hand for allergy season and your overall health and well-being.

Consider becoming a backyard beekeeper. Contact a local beekeeper and go for a tour to see if it is right for you. Some beekeepers look for property owners to "host" their bee hives in your backyard.

Sign petitions to ban the use of harmful insecticides. Many believe that pesticides can affect the central nervous system of the insects and suspect that they are partly responsible for the collapsing of the commercial beekeeper's colonies.

Whether it is stopping by your local organic farmers market, growing a bee friendly garden, eliminating insecticides, or just educating everyone you know around you about the importance of protecting and respecting our pollinators, every little bit helps.

"Feed your soul on Art and Nature; live by the sunlight and love by the moon."

– Amelia Dashwood

THE HONEY BEE PORTRAIT

Eat Healthier

Help Your Local Honey Bees

Shop at Local Organic Farms!

Shopping for organic fruits and vegetables at your local farm stands and markets can be a bit more costly. However, you are paying for food that will taste better, and will also be pesticide free and full of vitamins and minerals. You will also be supporting local organic farmers as well as helping the honey bees and other pollinators in your area. What a great way to take care of your health and the health of the planet at the same time.

Plants To Attract Bees To Your Garden

Borage	Coltsfoot	Milkweed
Echium	Coriander	Mint
Goldenrod	Cornflower	Poppy
Melissa/Lemon Balm	Elderberry	Rose Wild
Phacelia	Fireweed	Sunflowers
Black Locust	Hawthorne	Thyme
Asters	Hazelnut	Tulips, Old Species
Barberry	Heather	Valerian
Clover, White Sweet	Lavender	Veronica
Clover, Yellow Sweet	Linden	Willow

For more suggestions, check with your local nursery!

Bee Helpful

Bees work for man, and yet they never bruise

Their Master's flower, but leave it having done,

As fair as ever and as fit to use;

So both the flower doth stay and honey run.

– George Herbert, The Church-Providence

Chapter Six

Backyard Beekeeping

Backyard beekeeping is an excellent way to participate in helping save the honey bees. In turn, they will help your vegetable and flower gardens thrive as well as provide you with honey as an extra special reward.

In my journey to photograph and learn as much as I could firsthand about our remarkable pollinators, the honey bees, I ran across my lifelong friend Jill Brandt. She told me about her neighbor who was an urban beekeeper in a neighboring town only a few miles away.

Toni Bakker - Backyard Beekeeper

Just a few days later, Jill called me and informed me that her husband Ted said that the neighbor's bees were swarming and that I should come on over for a grand honeybee experience to document. After a quick equipment check to make sure I had all of my proper camera equipment, I slipped on my flip-flops and my sons David and Matthew rushed me over to the swarm for what turned out to be a marvelous experience of a lifetime.

When we arrived, the owner, Toni Bakker, greeted us with a welcoming smile. She approached us pulling a wagon filled with her beekeeping supplies. After quick introductions, she brought us over to the location of the honey bee swarm. My sons and

I were quite amazed. Honey bees were swarming, and there was an immense cluster of thousands of bees inside the branch of a pine tree. Toni explained that this was a natural, healthy occurrence and that the queen and her colony were in search of a new location possibly due to overcrowding in the hive. She also assured us that getting stung was highly unlikely because the bees are usually gentle during the swarm unless provoked.

We observed and I took photos as she fearlessly put on her gloves and proceeded to cut the branch out that held the swarm. After she cut the section out of the tree, she gently gave it a shake, and the queen and her colony got placed into their new hive.

A few weeks later, I sat down with Toni to get to know her and find out how she became involved in beekeeping. She resides in East Moriches, New York on the east end of Long Island. She said that she had an interest in bees all of her life and was intrigued by them. She found it especially fascinating how they are the only insect that provides food humans can consume.

Continued on Page 44

"A swarm of bees in May Is worth a load of hay;
A swarm of bees in June Is worth a silver spoon;
A swarm of bees in July is not worth a fly."
– An Old English Ditty

THE HONEY BEE PORTRAIT

Continued from page 42

As a young girl, Toni grew up spending summers in Greece where honey is a staple food, and she remembered always enjoying eating yogurt with honey. Toni also stated that her Mother taught her to respect insects and animals of all kinds. I asked Toni who her mentor was, and she replied, "the bees."

Toni lives a pretty busy life as a wife, career woman, and mother. However, beekeeping was on her "bucket list." About seven years ago, her daughter surprised her with a beekeeping kit to get her started as a birthday gift.

I also asked her how time-consuming beekeeping was for her. She told me a story of how she attended a beekeeping seminar a few years ago. Someone had asked the host just how much of her time and energy was involved in backyard beekeeping. She remembered the host replying that it was a little more work than taking care of a cat but less than taking care of a dog. That was an excellent way to put it into perspective.

After spending time with Toni, I saw how her respect and love for nature and her honey bees was very apparent. It seemed as though it was more than just a hobby for her. Tending to her bees did not appear to be a chore. Observing her with her hives and her bees was like watching someone care for beloved pets. She provides them with homes to live in and monitors them to make sure they are healthy. In return, they pollinate the landscape and provide her with nutritious honey.

From the honey and the beeswax the honey bees provide, Toni makes natural products such as lip balms, candles, and various size jars of pure honey.

Toni's entire family seems to enjoy keeping honey bees. While we were at the hives, her daughter, her nieces, and the family dog came by for a visit.

Deciding to keep honey bees is a commitment, and there is time involved, but the rewards are plentiful. Backyard Beekeeping is an exceptional option for anyone who has an interest in doing so. Before taking on such a commitment, one should first check with their local town government to make sure it is allowed in your neighborhood. It may also be a good idea to notify your neighbors and educate them on how their landscape will also benefit and assure them that there is nothing to fear.

A lot of space is not required to be a backyard beekeeper. In fact, many city dwellers have begun to keep bees up on rooftops, if allowed, in cities such as New York City.

There are many websites, as well as possible local beekeeper associations, that could offer assistance and guidance before considering if keeping bees is right for you. Spend a day with a backyard beekeeper, and soon you may be ordering your very own kit!

"Those bees, which chose thy sweet mouth for their hive, to gather honey from thy works, survive"

– Thomas Pecke, Parnassi Puerperium, 1659

"The keeping of bees is like the direction of sunbeams."

– Henry David Thoreau

Chapter 7
Ladies of Lavender

At first glance, you are visually captivated by the field that looks like a sea of blue and violet as you inhale the aromatic sweet scent of the lavender fragrance. As you take a closer look, you can see thousands of busy pollinators relentlessly working. They flit from flower to flower to feed on the nectar and spread pollen. Pollen is the sticky powder produced by the male part of the flower known as the stamen. The pistil of the flower that holds the seed is the female part. The sticky top is the stigma, and the seeds are in the ovule at the pistil's base.

As the honey bees, bumblebees, dragonflies, and other pollinators feed on the flowers, they move the sticky pollen to the stigma from the stamen and from flower to flower thereby inadvertently pollinating the plant and creating new seed production.

On the north fork of the east end of Long Island, New York is a 17-acre lavender farm called, "Lavender by the Bay" in the town of East Marion. The owners are Serge and Susan Rozenbaum.

Serge was kind enough to give me a tour of his apiary and allowed me to get a closer look at the hard-working ladies that play a large part in pollinating his 17 acres of majestic beauty so I could share it with you.

The honey bees of the lavender farm will not only pollinate the fields, but they will provide some of the most delicious and nutritious honey fresh from the hives. It is safe to roam through the plants along with the honey bees (and other pollinators) as long as you do not swat at them because their focus is to forage for food and are ordinarily harmless. They are, however, very protective of their hive, the queen, and their honey supply. Therefore, when in the vicinity of any honey bee hive, it is imperative that you wear protective equipment such as a beekeeper jacket, gloves, long pants, and shoes.

Next time you are in a field of flowers, take notice of the hard-working pollinators that beautify the world.

Thriving best in the sun, lavender is a lovely fragrant evergreen perennial herb that comes in different varieties and ranges in colors from white to purple-blue. It is known to have soothing and calming effects and is used in everything from baking, soaps, candles, perfumes, body and facial lotions, teas, aromatherapy treatments, and so much more. There is something so mentally and physically therapeutic about walking through a lavender field. Between the rows of striking color and the delightful aroma, the mind and body begin to relax and forget about whatever is causing stress in your life.

"The bee, from her industry in the summer, eats honey all the winter."

– Unknown

"A Bee is an exquisite Chymist" [chemist] "

– Royal Beekeeper to Charles II

"One can no more approach people without love than one can approach bees without care.

Such is the quality of bees..."

– Leo Tolstoy

"For bees, the flower is the fountain of life
For flowers,
the bee is the messenger of love."

– Kahlil Gibran

"A work of arte; and yet no arte of man,
Can worke, this worke, these little creatures can"

– Geffrey Whitney, 1586

"While walking through a field of flowers,
do not fear the honey bee...
Honor her and hold her sacred.
She is vital to the health of the
planet and all that inhabit it."

Nancy Ann 2017

Basic Beekeeping Tools

Some of the beekeeping tools that are basic are protective gear, a smoker to calm the bees, a brush, and a hive tool. The brush is used to gently removes the bees from the frame and protective gear. The hive tool helps to pry out the frames. It is also valuable to scrape off the propolis and wax from the beehive boxes.

Beekeeper

A beekeeper is a person who keeps and maintains honey bee colonies in hives. Some keep honey bees to pollinate their crops, for honey production and other commodities they provide, or just as a hobby. Honey bees not only provide essential pollination, but they also produce other valuable raw materials such as honey, royal jelly, beeswax, pollen, and propolis.

Three Main Elements of a Beehive

Workers

Queen

Drone

Honey Bee Anatomy

After smoking the beehive to calm the bees, the beekeeper is gently brushing the honey bees off the frame of the hive to take the honey and the beeswax for processing.

A location in the yard in which the beehives of the honey bees are placed and tended to is known as an apiary. Honey bees receive room and board in exchange for pollination of the crops and reward the landlord with precious honey.

So Much More Than Honey!

Since approximately 3000 BC, humans have also been using a substance honey bees provide called "propolis." It is considered to be of medicinal value. It is also called "honey bee glue." The bees make it from sticky plant resin.

They produce propolis by mixing beeswax and saliva with resin they gather from nature's sources such as tree sap. It is referred to as glue to the honey bees because they use it to seal in unwanted spaces in their hives. It is their homemade spackle to protect their living area.

Beekeepers use the hive tool to gently pry apart the frames from the hive that have been glued together by propolis as a sealant by the honey bees.

Worker honey bees use beeswax to make honeycomb cells. They have eight glands that produce wax.

Humans have been using beeswax for many products such as candles, cosmetics, pharmaceuticals, and so much more. It is another exceptional product provided by the busy honey bees.

"*The botanist should make interest with the bees if he would know when the flowers open and when they close*"

– Henry David Thoreau, 1906

"No bees, no honey; no work, no money."

– Unknown

About the Author

Nancy Ann Bowe is a graphic designer and photographer from the east end of Long Island, New York. After raising three sons, Robert, David, and Matthew, she went back to college to obtain her Bachelor of Fine Arts degree in Graphic Design. In May of 2014, she graduated as the class valedictorian proving that it is never too late to return to college to achieve a higher education.

For four years, Nancy Ann's photography focused mainly on macro photography of pollinators due to her intense interest in honeybees and bumblebees in particular. When she was completing her degree, her choice for the senior project/thesis for her was a no-brainer. She chose to photograph, design, and write this colorful book showcasing her photography and admiration of honey bees. She hopes to help educate the public on the importance of making our environment bee-friendly for them to continue to live and provide the planet with all they have to offer.

Sources

(n.d.). Retrieved 7 31, 2014, from The Melissa Garden: http://themelissagarden.com/TMG_Vetaley031608.htm

Facts About Honey Bees. (n.d.). Retrieved 8 4, 2014, from Back Yard Beekeepers Association: http://www.backyardbeekeepers.com/facts.html

Fruitless fall. new york: bloomsbury.Gough, A. (2008). THE BEE: PART 1 – BEEDAZZLED. Retrieved 8 4, 2017, from Andrew Gough: http://andrewgough.co.uk/articles_bee1/

Honey Please Don't Go. (n.d.). Retrieved 8 2, 2017, from Haagen-Dazs: http://www.haagendazs.us/Learn/HoneyBees/Jacobsen, R. (2008).

Jan Kingsbury, D. o. (n.d.). Häagen-Dazs® Honey Bee Haven: . Retrieved 8 2, 2014, from UC Davis College of Agricultural and Environmental Sciences : http://beebiology.ucdavis.edu/HAVEN/haagendazshbh.pdf

Karimi, F. (2014, 6 23). Obama Announces Plan to Save Honey Bees. Retrieved 7 29, 2014, from CNN Politics: http://www.cnn.com/2014/06/22/politics/honey-bees-protection/index.html

List of Pollinated Foods. (n.d.). Retrieved 8 4, 2014, from pollinator Partnership:http://pollinator.org/list_of_pollinated_food.htm

Pollination. (2009). Retrieved 8 3, 2014, from Missouri Botanical Garden: http://www.mbgnet.net/bioplants/pollination.html

Quotes About Bees (101 quotes). (n.d.). Retrieved August 26, 2017, from https://www.goodreads.com/quotes/tag/bees?page=2

Schacker, M. (2008). A spring without bees. Guilford, Connecticut:The Lyons Press.

Stipp, D. (2007). Flight of the honeybee. Fortune, 156((5)), 108-116.Wild for Bees. (2014). Retrieved 8 2, 2017, from Burt's Bees: http://www.burtsbees.com/Wild-For-Bees/wild-landing,default,pg.html

"Handle a book as a bee does a flower, extract its sweetness but do not damage it."

– John Muir

The artwork contains the text: "Protect Our Pollinators" and "PESTICIDES" and the signature "NANCYBOWE 2015"